Elephants

Victoria Blakemore

vblakemore.author@gmail.com

Copyright info/picture credits

Cover, nike159/Pixabay; Page 3, anujohanna/Pixabay; Page 5, skeeze/Pixabay; Page 7, roelroelofs/Pixabay; Page 9, delphinecourtes/Pixabay; Pages 10-11, tpsdave/Pixabay; Page 13, MrChris89/Pixabay; Page 15, magigigova/Pixabay; Page 17, nike159/Pixabay; Page 19, Dominique20/Pixabay; Page 21, NatureFreak/Pixabay; Page 23; MaudCuenin/Pixabay; Page 25, fuzzel2502/Pixabay; Page 27, AnteKante/Pixabay; Page 29, Andrea Izzotti/AdobeStock; Page 31, barnabas_lands/Pixabay; Page 33, nike159/Pixabay

Table of Contents

What Are Elephants?

Elephants are the largest land mammal. There are two kinds of elephants: the African elephant and the Asian elephant.

African elephants are larger than Asian elephants and all African elephants grow tusks.

Only male Asian elephants

grow tusks.

Size

African elephants can grow to be about thirteen feet long. They can weigh over 14,000 pounds.

Asian elephants are smaller. They can grow to be about ten feet long. They usually weigh less than 10,000 pounds.

Physical Characteristics

Elephants have large ears.

Their ears release heat from

their body. This helps to keep

them cool.

Elephant trunks have many

uses. They are used for

breathing, picking things up,

and greeting other

elephants.

Some elephants have tusks.

Their tusks can be used for

digging, lifting, and protecting

their trunk.

Habitat

Elephants are found in rainforests and **savannas**. They need areas with lots of plants for them to eat.

It is very hot and sunny where elephants live. They can use their trunk to spray water on their body. They also coat their skin in mud like a sunscreen.

Elephants are found on the
continents of Africa and Asia.

They are found in countries like Tanzania, China, Botswana, and India.

Diet

Elephants are **herbivores**.

They eat only plants. Their diet

is made up of grasses, leaves,

bamboo, bark, and roots.

Elephants can use their tusks

to tear pieces of bark off of

trees.

They use their trunk to pick up

plants and bring them to their

mouth.

Elephants use their trunks to get water. They suck up water with their trunk, then spray it into their mouth.

Since elephants are so large, they need a lot of food. Adult elephants can eat between 300 and 400 pounds of food each day!

Elephants spend most of their time

looking for food and eating.

Communication

Elephants have many ways that they can communicate. They make sounds like rumbles, roars, and cries.

They also use movement. An elephant that feels **threatened** may stand up tall and spread its ears to look bigger.

Elephants use their trunks to greet other elephants. They also use their trunks to comfort each other and play.

17

Movement

Elephants have very strong legs. They can walk long distances. Some elephants have been known to walk eighty miles in a day.

They can run at speeds of twenty-five miles per hour. This is only for short distances.

Elephants can swim to cross

rivers. They can use their trunk

like a snorkel if the water gets

too deep.

Herd Life

Elephants live in groups that are called herds. There are usually about twenty elephants in a herd.

A herd is run by the oldest female elephant. Herds travel together and look for food together.

Members of herds also protect

each other from predators.

Elephant Calves

Elephants usually have one baby. It is called a calf. Calves can weigh over 200 pounds when they are born.

The calf stays with its mother and the herd for years. The herd works together to protect calves from **predators**.

Calves do not know how to use their trunk yet. They sometimes suck on their trunk like a baby sucks on its thumb.

Characteristics

Elephants are very **intelligent** animals. They have a very good memory. They are thought to remember things from many years ago.

They have been known to show emotions such as sadness, joy, and anger.

Elephants form very close

bonds with members of their

herd.

Asian elephants are **endangered**. There are not many left in the wild. African elephants are listed as **vulnerable**. Their populations are **declining**.

Poaching for ivory and habitat destruction are the main threats facing habitats.

Elephants live for a long time.

They often live between fifty

and seventy years in the wild.

Circus Elephants

Elephants have performed in circuses for many years. Some people think that elephants should not have to perform in circuses.

Many circuses have stopped using elephants. Their elephants now live in special **preserves**.

Helping Elephants

There are many ways that people are trying to help elephants. Rangers **patrol** preserves to watch for **poachers**. They protect elephants from being killed for the **ivory** in their tusks.

Countries are setting up more preserves to provide elephants with a safe habitat.

Researchers are tracking elephant herds. They want to know where elephants go. That way, they can help to protect elephant habitats.

People are educating others about threats that elephants face. They hope that more people will want to help if they know about the problem.

Glossary

Declining: getting smaller

Endangered: at risk of becoming extinct

Herbivore: an animal that eats only plants

Intelligent: smart

Ivory: the hard, white material in elephant tusks

Patrol: to guard by making regular trips through

Poacher: someone who hunts animals against the law

Poaching: when animals are hunted against the law

Predator: an animal that hunts other animals for food

Preserves: areas of land set up to protect plants and animals

Savannas: plains that are covered with grass

Threatened: in danger

Vulnerable: when an animal is in danger of becoming endangered

About the Author

Victoria Blakemore is a first grade

teacher in Southwest Florida with a

passion for reading.

You can visit her at

www.elementaryexplorers.com

Also in This Series

Also in This Series

CPSIA information can be obtained
at www.ICGtesting.com
Printed in the USA
LVHW070616090222
710601LV00020B/1691